Tales from a Korean Maiden in America

Tales from a Korean Maiden in America

Dorothy M. Hong

iUniverse, Inc.
New York Lincoln Shanghai

Tales from a Korean Maiden in America

iUniverse, Inc.

For information address:
iUniverse, Inc.
2021 Pine Lake Road, Suite 100
Lincoln, NE 68512
www.iuniverse.com

ISBN: 0-595-28390-X

Printed in the United States of America

Contents

Non-Fiction Section

I May be Americanized 3

Vacationing on My Own 5

The Role of the Korean Church in My Life 8

Redefining My Political Identity 10

Finding God in My Greek Odyssey Years 13

Visiting My Native Homeland, Korea. 15

Dating. 17

Impact of Affirmative Action Plans on Koreans. 19

Looking Back to My Ancestral Land 22

Weekends without Visitors 26

A Book Review of Yi Sang's Nal Gae ("Wings") 28

The Korean Vernacular. 30

Caring for Autistic Child. 32

A Book Review of Don Oberdorfer's The Two Koreas 33

No Place Like ELM 35

Cheju Island 37

On Sexual Harassment 39

Korean Art at the MET. 41

Fiction section

Dead Person Does Not Speak 45

A Less Formidable Foe. 48

Meeting at the Clinic. 53

Acknowledgement

I would like to thank, first and foremost, iUniverse who made this publication possible. Also, I would like to thank Young Korean American Professional Network ("y-Kan") members, the main congregation and the English Language Ministry ("ELM") of the Korean Methodist Church & Institute and Alpha Phi Sorority members for their support in my publication efforts. Finally, I would like to thank the Korean Chamber of Commerce and Industry in USA, Inc. ("KOCHAM") and the Korean Cultural Service for their publications and referrals.

I made the following leaps from pencil scribbled note pad to word processor to Word Perfect to Microsoft computer since the summer of 1988 when I embarked on the task of writing in my room. With each leap I had the opportunity to transcribe and edit my writings which at first seemed tedious, but with each edited version coming to a fruition, my desire to publish my writings became stronger.

Some of my writings are extensions of my college senior honors thesis in Japanese and Korean history and literature, my independence study in the law school relating to criminology and evidentiary issues, my term papers on Black history in my A.P. history class in high school, along with my perusal of a fellow high school student's paper on Salem Witchcraft.

Affirmative Action, Sexual Harassment and Asian foreign languages were areas that I had labored on while I was active in student government in college and law school. To this end I would like to thank Cornell, University of Pennsylvania along with Brown and Harvard on their publications concerning Affirmative Action Programs for Asians and Sexual Harassment Surveys and Studies.

Korean Yang Ban (Aristocracy) history is something that is uniquely my own family history as my linage may be traced to Yang Ban status in both my paternal and maternal sides. It is not unusual for a person of Korean descent to boast of Aristocratic heritage in one's ancestry, but a few can actually trace Yang Ban lineage following the Yi Dynasty's laws.

I tend to think that Koreans are most open-minded about Europeans since it is a direct neighbor of Russia and it had a long history of small number of European invaders lurking in the Korean shores and borders. These invaders were soon captivated by the landscape, the distinct four seasons, the splendid culture and its robust inhabitants and later these invaders were subdued and found themselves mere sojourners, but some had been completely absorbed by the native Korean population, leaving only a faint hint of European features in an otherwise Mongolian face in certain sections of the Korean peninsula. But I defer to other opinions that Chinese may be the most broad-minded about Europeans or that Japanese may be the friendliest to Europeans.

Koreans see America as an extension of the European civilization, but instead they find overwhelming complexities and astonishing differences upon their having lived through the American experience. My goal is to add my voice in the definition of America.

Non-Fiction Section

✦

Eighteen (18) Articles from Korean American Newsletters

I May be Americanized

by Dorothy Hong
Edited Article First Published in Spirit of y-Kan,
Volume 5, Number 9, May 1994 Issue

Upon finishing school, I came back to New York to live with my parents. I had kept in touch with a couple of my neighbors from school, but by and large sharing space with people who were unrelated to me was an unpleasant experience. My first roommate at school was Korean which gave me a measuring rod to differentiate the extent of racial and other differences that had impacted our lives. The first Korean woman was tall and attractive, so I imagined that I would run into a problem where we may have to compete for the same man, particularly Korean man. Notwithstanding her physique, the kind of social interaction with men in comparison with my white Jewish neighbor was nothing.

When I went to my graduate single dorm with an adjoining bathroom with my mother and aunt, I found myself explaining my neighbor's rather promiscuous behavior. The first night my neighbor moved in, she invited a man over to her room. We all heard them giggling until three in the morning. This kind of behavior went on rather frequently way into the final examination time. Granted that she later acquired a boyfriend and in her custom it is acceptable to sleep with her boyfriend, I still recall her screams of pleasure at four in the morning which initially alarmed me.

Having come from a family where baby making was exclusively a husband-wife venture with occasional allowance for birth control, I wondered what my neighbor must have gone through in her mind having multiple sexual partners. She seemed to be handling both the emotional and physical consequences well though.

To her, she could not resist sexual attraction with an available man. She had to perform sex as if she was entitled to it since she was an adult. To her, premarital sex does not pose any impediment to her later quest in acquiring a desirable mate for a life of marriage. To her, sex is like eating food. To her, the fact that she is engaging in such acts is a signal that she is healthy, attractive and socially acceptable to the Gentile world.

Fortunately, the extent of noise emitting from my white neighbor did not come to the level of nuisance to the extent that I would have a cause for a lawsuit. We simply had different lifestyles and different priority agenda.

I admire successful Jewish population for their ability to penetrate into the mainstream culture particularly in New York City through their intelligence, hard work, ability and creativity.

Premarital sexual promiscuity, however, is not something I wish to digest into my lifestyle and make it into my own New World culture. There is a limitation as to the extent of assimilation with dominant culture in New York City even if such promiscuity is condoned by Hollywood movies when I feel strongly that such a cultural element is not compatible with my physical constitution and it may even prove to be hazardous to health in light of all those venereal diseases including AIDS.

Vacationing on My Own

by Dorothy Hong
Edited Article First Published in CrossRoads
Volume 9 Number 4 September 1995 Issue

The idea of going on a vacation on my own seemed exciting. But, at the same time, a sense of concern crept into my mind because of the possible risks involved. Safety now a days is a concern for both women and men, but especially for women. Notwithstanding these factors, I felt ready as I had wanted to do this for a long time. So, for the first time in my life I took a vacation by myself.

I remember going on an overnight trip to Kyoto in Japan with my dance troupe in my elementary school days[1]. I had a difficulty sleeping with ten other girls in the same tatami floored room and putting up with my teacher's scary story about a human blood-sucking black rose. I had come a long way since that trip, adding to my list sleep away camps, dorm life and overnight stays at relatives' and girl-friends' houses.

A unique feature about this trip was that I was going to an unknown place to do new things. They say that one can strip away all pretenses and come to terms with one's true character when going to an unknown place full of strangers. So, this was a test for me, a chance to rediscover myself.

I went on a group package vacation to Ocean City, Maryland and thereafter stopped off at Chesapeake Bay and Cape May. When I saw my fellow travel mates in the bus, I was instantly put at ease. They were mostly women: widows who had met each other at a therapy for those mourning for their deceased spouses; mother and daughter pairs; and girlfriends from work who wanted to get away from their respective family obligations.

---

1. At the time, I attended a private Korean elementary school while residing in Tokyo with my family.

We lodged at a large first rate hotel overlooking the Atlantic Ocean. For the next few days I went along with the itinerary set by the tour director, such as sightseeing, taking pictures, going to museums, and eating crabs. I spent my free time beachcombing in the mornings, sunbathing in the afternoons and swimming in the indoor swimming pool in the evenings.

The view of the waves and the horizon was breathtaking in the morning and I felt overwhelmed by the fact that somewhere across the horizon lay another Continent and civilization. Of course, centuries ago Europeans came to this land by ship, landed on this very shore, determined to make a new home for themselves in this land. Thinking of the insurmountable obstacles in the high seas and other hardships those Europeans must have confronted while on board their ship, I felt lucky to have come to this country in an air-conditioned airplane, in plush seats with other amenities in a matter of hours.

Feeling the small and gentle waves rolling in toward the beach shore on my legs and gazing into the ocean, I forgot all my worries and petty concerns and even forgot for a moment about my parents, who at the time were vacationing in Mainland China.

But at night in my hotel room, when I was alone with a copy of Allan Bloom's Love and Friendship, a weight descended down on my shoulders when I realized that I was entirely alone and responsible for my well being until the dawn. I double locked everything, kept a small light on and called home each night to keep in touch with my brother and to hear about my parents from him.

I relished the idea of being alone, but I looked forward to getting together with my family later. In their absence, I was reminded of the sense of security, trust and love that they had instilled in me.

On the last day I found out that one of my travel mates had broken her arm while ice skating in the hotel and had had to leave separately on her own to go to a nearby hospital. An elderly gentleman in the bus informed me that another travel mate had undergone a series of surgeries and physical therapies to completely rebuild his arms and legs. I considered myself fortunate for not braking any bones, and I felt thankful for the things modern technology and medicine could provide.

This vacation afforded me a chance to relax, contemplate our own civilization and briefly meet with individuals striving to be happy dealing with their own problems.

The Role of the Korean Church in My Life

by Dorothy Hong
Edited Article First Published in CrossRoads
Volume 9 Number 5, November 1995 Issue

I was baptized when I was eleven, only six months after I had set foot in America. That is not to say that I was totally new to the Christian way of life. My family and I celebrated Christmas in Korea and a couple of times I accompanied my grandmother to evening services. Having come to a new land composed of diverse races and different languages, I immediately clung to Christianity to find a new way to be and to be filled spiritually with God's blessings and wonders.

It was a combination of God's grand spectrum of love and his wrath that gave me a sense of control in what often seemed a chaotic life in America. I was initially drawn to a Korean church because of my limited command of English. I also felt a tinge of nostalgia. By going to a monochromic Korean church each week, I felt close to my old Korean society and all the simplicity and naiveté that were associated with my childhood days there.

The Korean church life afforded me a chance to let my hair down occasionally and compare notes with other Korean Americans who were similarly situated when confronted with a range of issues.

After learning that other Christians in American history, such as Pilgrims and black slaves, had overcome hardships and had found a more enriching life here on this earth, as well as a peaceful and everlasting life in heaven, through worship and practice, I became convinced that God would hear my prayers if I were zealous in my Christian practice.

Believing in Jesus Christ was much easier than actually practicing his teachings on a day to day basis. But I have been working hard at forgiving others who have wronged me.

My faith in Jesus Christ and God made me aware, at the same time, of the existence of Satan. In times of weariness and distress, there were moments when I felt as though the devil was initiating me. In those moments, I was disturbed by the notion of erotic and vindictive witches who had conspired with Satan. As I recall, those were the times when I was so preoccupied with mundane issues that I was lackadaisical in my church attendance.

Feeling frazzled, I sought refuge in the Korean church. Over and over again, I had asked God for forgiveness for all the ugly things I had dwelled upon which debilitated my spiritual growth. I felt comfort in Christian fellowship and I sought the gentle company of other Korean American Christians even though by then, I no longer had to struggle with the English language. I managed to be in good spirit again by downscaling my workload, doing good work, volunteering in my neighborhood and becoming little bit more selective about whom I came to associate with.

After my trials, I learned to take risks in forgiving and loving others. I see the devil lurking in my Christian life and am determined to chase it away. Now I am ten times more thankful to God and Jesus Christ than I have ever been for giving me the inner strength to cope with tribulations.

Redefining My Political Identity

by Dorothy Hong
Edited Article First Published in CrossRoads
Volume 11 Number 1, March 1996 Issue

By and large politicians and politics have had little impact on my personal decisions. But through my participation in the political process I have come to redefine my individual identity from being a Korean, when I first arrived in this country, to being an American citizen.

Back in South Korea, the only time I became politically aware of my identity was when I attended a grand opening of a Children's Theme Park in Seoul. President Park Chung Hee was going to give a speech at that momentous occasion. I was selected to be one of the few students from my elementary school to attend the ribbon cutting ceremony. We were told to look presentable since we might be on T.V. In retrospect, the idea of dressing up seems ludicrous since children usually go to an amusement park to play.

Throughout my school days here in America I was indifferent to the aspirations of American politicians. For pragmatic reasons, however, I became a naturalized American citizen in my senior year of high school. Although I was not interested in the "American Politics," I was active in student government during my undergraduate and law school days. Even as an American citizen, however, most of my peers and teachers viewed me as a Korean or a hyphenated Korean-American, at best, and rarely as an American.

Kim Dae Jung[1], the Korean political dissident and a perennial hopeful candidate for the Presidency came to visit Cornell in my senior year. When I asked Mr. Kim how Korean American students would be able to help enhance human rights in Korea, Mr. Kim interpreted my question as being an academic one. He saw me

---

1.   Kim Dae Jung later served as the President of South Korea.

as a foreign American who had once been a Korean but who had deliberately left Korea to look for a better life elsewhere.

In my second year of University of Pennsylvania Law School, the Dean of the school assigned me to an extra advisee, a Korean LLM student. The Korean LLM student struck me as a quiet and dignified man of wealth. Even after many lunches and dinners at the law school cafeteria, he never mentioned his parents. I found out later that his father had been the Mayor of Seoul. I learned this information from a chauffeur who drove me back after a lunch with my former advisee when I was in Korea one summer. I was not surprised by the information and in retrospect I would not have treated him any differently had I known that he was the Mayor's son. But the fact that my former advisee obviously considered such an information irrelevant to me was amusing.

After finishing school I came back to New York and registered myself as a Democrat. I liked the view held by the Democratic Party of looking at the society bottom up and of nurturing people who contribute to our society by working with their hands.

One day I came across Thomas Kean's autobiography in the local Public Library. His writings made me consider whether Republications would be beneficial to minorities and women as well. I volunteered to help out with Rudy Giuliani's NYC mayoral campaign, after feeling disillusioned with Mayor Dinkins. The work I did at the campaign headquarter was tedious, but I felt so strongly about reducing racial tensions and the crime rate in the City that the Party lines seemed trivial.

In my next campaign involvement with Mario Cuomo's NYS gubernatorial campaign, Asian Americans were considered a group to be reckoned with and special campaign efforts were made to court Asian voters. After hearing Governor Cuomo speak at a fund raiser dinner in Chinatown for Asian Americans and again at the Korean Chu Sok (Harvest) Festival in Flushing Meadow Park, I felt thrilled to be part of the dynamic American society. His speeches recognized the fact that immigrants bring their long history and culture to enrich rather than replace the American culture.

My sense of American citizenship became stronger after serving as a volunteer for Cuomo's and Giuliani's campaigns. I am glad to be part of a great nation blessed with so many natural as well as man-made wonders. As a card carrying member of Democratic National Committee I am deeply committed to the ideals held by the American founding fathers. I look forward to witnessing fellow Korean Americans seeking high ranking public offices some day.

Finding God in My Greek Odyssey Years

by Dorothy Hong
Edited Article First Published in CrossRoads
Volume 15 Number 1 August 1996 Issue

In my sophomore year of college at Cornell, I joined a sorority on campus. I had been putting off my joining a sorority until my sophomore year because I was contemplating to transfer to another school in my freshman year. A couple of other Korean girls from my high school had already joined different sororities in their freshman year. One joined Sigma Delta Tau, a sorority which was initially founded for Jewish women, and another joined Kappa Kappa Gamma, the one that was mentioned in an American classic novel, <u>Vanity Fair</u>. The sorority which I finally joined was Alpha Phi, an old established international sorority[1] with a big house on campus, but that which was not considered as a "clone house," that is to say, the most popular house on campus.

My sorority house provided me a nurturing atmosphere to grow as a mature woman. Particularly in my sophomore and junior years, it gave me a sense of "home away from home," punctuating my grueling academic life with good food, warm friends, lively discussions, interesting parties and worthwhile philanthropic activities. It was a place where I hung out when I didn't feel like studying, where I brought faculty members for tea and dinner, and where I stayed when all the dorms were closed. I had fun during my pledge days singing Alpha Phi songs at the house and going to another fraternity house at five in the morning in one cold February morning in Ithaca with another pledge to remove a big wooden Greek sign to have a party with them. The strong Greek system at Cornell also served as a "nerve center" of academic resources and a "networking headquarter" for all other political and social activities on campus.

---

1. Alpha Phi has chapters in Canada.

I have kept in touch with a few of my sorority sisters after my graduation from college, and had helped out with a chapter at Columbia University[2] upon my coming back to New York. Although my sorority does not boast of "celebrity" alumni such as Sandra Day O'Connor and Elizabeth Dole of Delta Delta Delta, Alpha Phi women are God fearing women, analogous more to a turtle than a bunny in a race.

Despite prejudices that existed against Asians while I was in college, I still got a lot out of my sorority experience. Throughout my college days as an active woman of Alpha Phi, I was appreciative of the Hellenic reasoning and camaraderie. Each one of us is a god in some small ways if one works hard at it, but I am convinced that there is one God who knows all and who does not hesitate his show of love.

---

2.   I learned at the Founder's Day meeting in October 2002 held in New York City that the chapter at Columbia University closed.

Visiting My Native Homeland, Korea

by Dorothy Hong
Edited Article First Published in Sprit of y-Kan,
Volume 7 Number 3, November 1996 Issue

The Korea I left behind more than two decades ago had developed dramatically as evidenced by my visits in 1986 and this year 1996. The most pronounced change that I observed was in retail business. The familiar scene of Seoul in the 70's of the open markets filled with pudgy and overly solicitous "ajumma" in colorful and patterned garbs was replaced by tall glassy department store buildings filled with lithe young women in crisp uniforms, helpful yet somewhat staid in their approach to the customers.

My ten day stay in Korea was like a dream, meandering about towns without ever getting lost and gliding from one event after another with neither my diary book nor wrist watch. I was amazed at how much I was able to accomplish during my short stay: attending functions to commemorate my ancestors, visiting relatives, sightseeing and shopping. The memories of my stay in Korea are vivid and detailed now, but later they will be assisted by snapshots and videos that were taken during my stay.

The magical and charming juxtaposition of the old and traditional with the modern and contemporary found everywhere in Korea made me aware of the interplay between the great weight of five thousand year old Korean civilization withered by invasions and the dynamics of international free market in which South Korea had slowly but steadily gained acceptance as an undeniable force.

The gatherings with my relatives turned out to be scenes more reminiscent of some far-out off Broadway plays rather than the scene I had dreaded in my mind before my arrival in Korea of a boring bunch adhering to rigid decorum, asking me questions such as "When are you getting married?"

One clear evening, as I took a leisurely walk in Myungdong in Seoul, I saw many carefree young Korean couples having a good time and enjoying each other's company over a cup of coffee or noodle. In a matter of a couple of hours drive from Myungdong, however, stood an ominous reminder of the divided Korea, Pan Moon Jum. It was at Pan Moon Jum that visitors were warned that even a slight signal or an unkempt hair could be interpreted as a dangerous sign by the North Korean soldiers on the other side of Korea.

The following morning after my arrival in Korea, when I was out on the street, I felt as though I never left Korea. But when I picked up a newspaper, I was unable to comprehend a featured story on my great-grand father, an Independence Movement Leader[1], due to my limited ability to read Chinese characters. Ironically, my Korean heritage alone was not sufficient to enable me to integrate as a fellow Korean citizen in South Korea, a nation of capitalism and democracy modeled after the United States where I grew up.

---

1.   My great-grand father, a lawyer, served as the President of the Provisional Korean Government in China during the Japanese Occupation Period in Korea.

Dating

by Dorothy Hong
Edited Article First Published in Spirit of y-Kan
Volume 7 Number 6, February 1997 Issue

At some point during schooling a Korean in America confronts a choice of dating a non-Korean. This question of dating someone who is considered an "out group" is more significant to a person of Korean extraction than to a white American since Koreans make up a small percentage of the racial minority group in this country. Unfortunately, due to the Korean War from the 1950's, we have an ugly reminder of the term "Yang Galbo" referring to those catering to Westerners[1]. Such a term seems misnomer now, in light of interracial dating and marriages we know of and inter-racial pairing in the media. Most notably, we hear of the wedding announcements of mixed race couples in the society columns of newspapers.

A Korean in America considers two options in her dating journey: either pursue Korean gatherings to find a Korean guy to date or go out with those few who are interested in Asians in the mainstream society. To me, the term "dating" refers to a social activity with an individual, a time spent together to air out views and test out likings that are personal in nature. Ultimately, I would like to be matched with one who is similarly situated, or, alternatively, with one whose association would be symbiotic.

Although I have dated more Korean men than Caucasian and Chinese men, and others combined, I think that the elements of courtship remain unchanged in any relationship. They are as follows: (1) respecting the other person's heritage, occupation, and hobbies; (2) maintaining self-respect; (3) maintaining personal space;

---

1. Yang Galbo literally means those poverty stricken young women who turned to prostitution for American G.I.'s stationed in South Korea.

(4) building tolerance; (5) avoid making each other sick or enraged; and (6) enjoying each other's company.

As a Christian, I am aware of the following passage in the New Testament, "Thou shall not yoke with non-believers." The New Testament, therefore, affords the possibility of a relationship based upon Christ's teaching of love in an otherwise tenuous association marked by measurable differences and doubts. We heard of the saying, "Love conquers all."

This does not mean that a Christian would make a more desirable mate. Many relationships purportedly founded upon love are misguided by perceptions based on hostility, ignorance and lie. Nevertheless, by his upholding to practice Christianity my date and I would have a common ground to build a relationship.

Impact of Affirmative Action Plans on Koreans

by Dorothy Hong
Edited Article First Published in Sprit of y-Kan
Volume 8 Number 11, July 1998 Issue

The United States government became the major instrument to take positive measures to redress what they perceived as historical misconducts in depriving people of color various opportunities and privileges they would otherwise have been entitled had it not been for the visceral impact of their features separating them from the majority race of the United States, the white citizens of European descents, who had enjoyed over four hundred years of all amenities of first class citizenship of America such as voting, owning property, freedom of press and religion, freedom of movement and otherwise enjoy society and participate in community while able to make a living and have a family.

These were deprived to the people of color, including Koreans. There were a few Mulattos and other "polluted" Negroes who were able to obtain a substantial wealth because of their "bastard" status which won much sympathy among certain white slave owners during the antebellum period.

The major obstacle Koreans face as a set back in comparison to the white race is that Koreans had been prohibited from lawful entry into this country in significant number until recently towards the end of the 20th century. When asked the "early" Korean immigrants where they sat in the bus before Martin Luther King, Jr. became famous, Koreans unanimously answered "We were seated with all other coloreds, the Negroes." Whatever adversities blacks complained through legal means, Koreans had also silently suffered.

Recently, the U.S. government not only monitored unlawful discriminations, but also implemented special economic programs to make up for the past wrongdoings that were associated with government funded institutions. Namely, universities formed affirmative action programs to foster benevolent image of large, well established American institutions.

There were complaints from other minority groups, especially from blacks that the Affirmative Action programs had disproportionately benefited Asians; benefits which blacks bitterly argue that they alone fought while other Asians remained reticent. A few black administrators even went further with this argument, proclaiming economic achievements of Asians and high standardized scores achieved by Asians which make Affirmative Action programs unnecessary for the "Model Minority." Asian students, especially Koreans, which make up for the largest first generation immigrant group on college campuses since the seventies, took offence to this stance by the "acceptable and successful" BASP's, the Black Anglo Saxon Protestants.

The "enlightened" black administrators' argument works like this: because blacks are the only racial minority that bears the dual burden of having to overcome past remnants of being chained slaves to white American citizens and otherwise overcome other societal handicaps and challenges that other racial minorities had inherited as well and whose stigmatization they all still suffer, blacks should be the only recipient of Affirmative Action programs.

Furthermore, because blacks have historically provided indispensable services and labor to white people, the United States government should make a special preferential treatment toward blacks by isolating them from the racial classification and handing out to blacks the primary choice, if not the only choice to entitle them to Affirmative Action programs. Because of alarming evidence of increasing hostilities, if not violence toward Asians, particularly Koreans in black ghetto areas, largely due to Koreans' envious drive and work ethics which enabled them to achieve relatively more economic success in comparison to blacks in the same areas, blacks perceive that this is the opportune time to rid of Asians from such remedial programs altogether. Blacks use ill feelings articulated towards Asians as a tool to get closer to white people so that blacks may obtain legal racial classification different and superior to other racial minorities because blacks are the only racial minority who have enjoyed a long American history under the same roof with whites.

Asian activists and legislators should be wary of such "red herring" arguments put forward thus far from the black community. Without a thorough review of legislative history and jurisprudence, Koreans and other Asians may end up being "food" to blacks who see America as their own "Promised Land" from God.

Looking Back to My Ancestral Land

by Dorothy Hong
Edited Article First Published in Spirit of y-Kan
Volume 8 Number 10, June 1998 Issue

I spent my infancy in Taegu in Kyngsang Bukdo Province of South Korea. My parents had temporarily stayed in that area because my father had a teaching post in a college there. That province is known for beautiful women and the legend has it that all babies born there are fair skinned. Aversion of dark skinned person in Korea traces back to the theory that they are too rough and strong. Fair skin is associated with purity and cleanliness. It is also associated with an aristocratic element, because peasants work out in fields, but aristocrats do not.

That province is not an unfamiliar terrain as both my father's and my mother's linage may be traced to towns in that area. There are cities and towns where their clans still reside in that area. My paternal grandmother was born and had grown up there until my grandmother married my grandfather. By comparison to American towns, they have ethos similar to the Midwest.

The capital of Silla Dynasty in BC era is in this province. It is a section of Korea much known for its folklore and mythology, and rich culture and custom.

Most of the aristocrats from the Yi Dynasty which lasted about five hundred years until the Japanese Occupation in the 20th century can still trace their ancestry in this province. For example, Andong Kim, Andong Kwon, Poongsan Hong, Milyang Sohn, Koryung Shin, just to name a few, are prominent aristocratic clans from this region. The "bone" aristocrats of Silla Dynasty who were related to Pak (translation meaning White) royal family is different from the largely meritocratic and southeast and south of capital Seoul region centered aristocrats of Yi Dynasty known as the "Yangban." Yi Dynasty's aristocracy is construed to have meritocratic elements because whoever achieves passing score on government sponsored civil servant examinations and be appointed to a high post may be considered an aristocrat. In general, an aristocrat marries another aristocratic family member. After third generation of not attaining "Yangban" rank, he would have to step down to a gentry level and is no longer considered an aristocrat unless the family then recoups by passing a battery of examinations and attains a position. A prejudice persisted against applicants of furthest northern region in Korea. Supposedly, the founder of Yi Dynasty dwelled in that region before mobilizing to found Yi Dynasty and he felt insecure about their loyalty toward him and his dynasty. Although majority of the Yangabn was from the south of Seoul, Yangban from the north of Seoul was not non-existent.

During Yi Dynasty no aristocrats however high their positions were allowed to amass wealth greater than the royalty. This applied to the size of their estate which was surveyed periodically and its finding must be less than the royalty's. In addition, an aristocrat may be asked to move from one location to another depending on where he is appointed by its kingdom. During the months where the high ranking officer aristocrats meet in the Capital they are separated from their immediate family members who often reside in other regions. Aristocrats may have multiple residences in the aristocratic section of the neighborhood where aristocrats live and work exclusively. The household servants and slaves live in the same estate homes as the head of the household. A judge (an aristocrat by title) may have his own custody area where he keeps outlaws in jail. Incidentally, an aristocrat one day who is convicted as a traitor may be asked to become a slave another day, but a slave may earn freedom from his bondage with a payment of bond. High government posts aristocrats are the most affluent population beside the royalty.

Aristocrats also paint, and write especially poetry. Often when aristocrats socialize they exchange poetry in a secluded private garden. They like to hunt, ride horse, do archery, or have an academic interest in nature. An entertainment also includes female dancer, singer and tea and wine server. However, to be a mistress of duration of an aristocrat tolerated by his family members, the mistress must boast of similar social ranking.

Among aristocrats, there is a ranking system between civil and military aristocrats. The civil aristocrats are ranked higher than warriors are. Envoys to China to pay tribute to the Emperor of China among many emperors, lord of lords, so to speak, for diplomatic and trade reasons were selected from aristocrats. Korea and Vietnam were part of the tributary system, but Japan was not. The purpose of the Tributary System was mainly to keep peace with neighbors, stemming from a notion shared by its participants to rid "Barbarians" from their territories. It was believed that Barbarians might be seeking to invade Korea, Vietnam or China. The chief barbarians documented in Korean history were Mongolians and Japanese. Other documented invasions by ship, which was much smaller in scale, were led by French.

Korean race is considered a Mongolian race. Mongolians are yellow people from Asia, known for their thick straight hair, small nose and prominent cheekbones. Mongolian feature tends to be more associated with swarthy peasant/farmer stock as oppose to more refined and delicate Chinese stock mainly because the Chinese cheekbones are not as prominent in the same Asian flat face as compared to Caucasian race. The opulent Orient of the past considered by Korea also includes as Orientals the inhabitants of Mediterranean, Middle East, North Africa and India in addition to Asia. Although Native Americans may have migrated from Asia, they are not considered as Oriental. Japanese has a long history of kidnapping Koreans to Japan to transplant culture which is influenced by China. Japanese and Koreans are considered one race. Japanese aristocrats may trace their linage to Korean aristocrats. The migration pattern from the bygone days show that the present inhabitants of Japan may trace their roots to Koreans from the Southeast section of the Korean peninsula. But until recently, Japanese did not want to be associated with Koreans, feeling which became widespread since Japanese Occupation in Korea and rapid modernization of Japan by Western standards. Japanese aristocrats are different from Korean aristocrats in that Japanese can only be an aristocrat by birth.

Manchurian section had originally been part of Korea's Koguryo kingdom, but Korean had lost its land to China when the Silla kingdom sought military assistance from the China's Tang kingdom to unify Silla with Korea's other kingdoms, Paekjae and Koguryo. Paekjae and Koguro and Silla merged together into Silla, which became the surviving kingdom, which thereafter became Koryo kingdom in BC era. The word Korea may be traced back to European trade activities with Koryo dynasty. It is a mispronunciation of Koryo, which sounded like Korea.

European recognized Korea's architecture, pottery, embroidery and its development of Chinese medicine and Confucius and Manchius teachings. Various Chinese kingdoms recognized Korean scholarship of classical Chinese learning.

Korea's widespread use of many metals and printing press and astrological equipments, certain fabrics, farming techniques as well as the use of mirror precedes such usages in Europe. Mongolian invasion of Europe may have attributed to such same usages in Europe later as well.

Weekends without Visitors

by Dorothy Hong
Edited Article First Published in Spirit of y-Kan
Volume 9 Number 2, October 1998 Issue

An unprecedented number of front page news featured South Korea recently. Unfortunately, the news sets a chill as an economic debacle swept across East Asia, Korea being one of the hardest hit nations. Guests from Korea who used to fill my weekend agenda are a thing of the past. Comments like "We have this in Korea too," or "You shouldn't have immigrated. Everybody is rich back home," now seem echoes of the past.

The rumor has it that even with an infusion of IMF aid to South Korea, Korean consumers are not buying American products. Korea which had been a source of refuge and inspiration to so many Korean immigrants seems to have dwindling force at this time in the psyche of Koreans in America. To hear that Korea which had vitally shaped my thinking and eating habit has somewhat lost its sense of identity seems a shame. Korea's strong sense of identity was shaped by its remarkable economic achievement in the 20th century Euro-centric free market world, with America being the central figure for Korea. With so many shops winding down and mergers, a noble cause like patriotism seems to lose its momentum there. Boycotting American goods is not an act of patriotism. Rather it betrays a feeble identity of Korea's not knowing whom to side in times of economic turmoil.

If Koreans in Korea feel this way, I wonder about the repercussions abroad. Korean immigrants are resigned to the fact that there is no place to go back if things don't work out here. The alternatives and options to disillusioned and weary Korean immigrants have been drastically limited.

Yet I am optimistic that Korea will come out of the slump as Korea had proven to be a nation of faith and resilience. I look forward in the future to have my Korean friends visit New York. Their past snooty attitude toward a workaholic immigrant like me now seems harmless. I miss them. When they come back for a visit, I want to show them all that I have come to appreciate in America however short a time they will have stayed here. After all America is dependent on Korean consumerism of American products.

A Book Review of Yi Sang's Nal Gae ("Wings")

by Dorothy Hong
Edited Article First Published in Spirit of y-Kan
Volume 9 Number 4, December 1998 Issue

Yi Sang's short story Nal Gae ("Wings") was written during the Japanese Occupation period in the turn-of-the century in the Korean peninsula. Wings is a fiction based on Yi Sang's own living arrangement with his girlfriend for a brief period.

The narrator speaks of his idle life, deprived of title, job and family, living together with a female companion who sleeps in an adjoining bedroom. Having nothing to do during the day, he goes to his girlfriend's bedroom and plays with her toiletries on her vanity table sniffing cosmetics and perfumes. At other times he spends his waking hours alternating in different positions in his bed.

One afternoon he sees his girlfriend fornicating with a stranger. After the intruder leaves the room, the girlfriend hands over her prostitution money to the narrator. Catching sadness in her eyes, later the narrator runs to the out house toilet and there he proceeds to throw down the heavy piggybank and all the prostitution money in it into the latrine.

Thereafter he gets an incredible headache. He checks his girlfriend's vanity table for a medication, but he is befuddled by an English label on the pill bottle. He gets suspicious as to whether the medication is for headache or something else, and decides not to take the pill.

The story ends with narrator's having an uncontrollable urge to throw himself down from a tall building, feeling like a stuffed genius; he feels paralyzed to do anything in life.

The story gives a bleak reality of the colonial period, a healthy Korean man being marginalized, deprived of livelihood, thereby stripping away his masculine identity and rupturing the very social fabric of the patriarchal Korean society.

The story also portrays a woman being dehumanized and made unworthy, as she is made unmarriageable, unable to procreate with her husband and raise her children in a family setting. For a woman of her age, the optimal economics is her having to direct her energy for her nucleus family.

Japanese colonialist continued to assume and justify their actions against Koreans, calling them "too stupid to make self-determinations" until they were confronted with Korea's organized Independence Movements, most notably the March 1st Movement.

The Korean Vernacular

by Dorothy Hong
Edited Article First Published in Sprit of y-Kan
Volume 8 Number 6, January 1998 Issue

I had a training in the Korean language until the fifth grade when I came to an English-speaking country, the United States of America. As a high school student I did a presentation of Korean alphabet, Hangul, which included posters of my own handwriting of Korean alphabet. The audience commented that certain characters were reminiscent of certain Hebrew characters, such as "kiok" and flip side of "digut" and a Greek motif which looked like "lear". These comments triggered in my mind the extent of contacts that the Korean peninsula had enjoyed throughout their trade activities under the rule of various kingdoms before South Koreans became fanatic about learning English in the 20th century.

I had read from several sources that the Korean vernacular language is most closely related to the present day Japanese spoken language. The Korean language belongs to Altaic-Tungustic tongue whose grammar and pronunciation are most similar to Japanese. Such a tongue may be directly traced to Mongolian and Siberian dialects. The vestiges of the classical Korean expressions and oral histories indicate a distinct passage of social intercourse with Mediterranean and Nordic civilizations, mainly those of Turkey and Finland.

The classical Korean learning, on the other hand, shows that the etymology of widely used vocabularies are traced to the standard Chinese written characters. Mastering Chinese characters was an indispensable part of classic education and the only route to earning government posts until the end of Yi dynasty.

Earning high post within the Korean government was a way to earning a title of aristocracy aside from marrying into the aristocracy during the Yi dynasty. In this way, the "Yangban," caste system, the aristocracy of the Yi Dynasty, was construed to have a meritocratic element. Within the caste system, Yangban consisting of scholar/ruler was at the top, then came farmer, then artisan and the last was merchant. Other common people did not belong to the caste system.

With the introduction of Hangul, the official Korean phonetic alphabet, during the early Yi Dynasty, common people were able to enjoy reading and writing as a day-to-day routine matter without having to incur costly private tutor expense to master tons of Chinese written characters.

Today, Hangul is the backbone of written communication in Korean language. The use of Chinese characters in the written discourse still remains however. An analogy may be made between the use of Latin in the Anglo-Saxon language and the use of Chinese characters in the Korean language. The use of written Chinese characters, however, is more prevalent in Korea as they are still used in daily newspapers and store signs in South Korea.

In today's economy Koreans learn English to remain competitive in the global market. Learning how to speak and write English has become part of the curriculum in the various levels of school. Koreans rely on the English pronunciation of many things of Western origin in the Korean language. For instance, RADIO is spelled phonetically similar spelling to the same Western word instead of a translation of such a Western electronic devise into something completely Korean.

Aside from the integration of a certain few English words into Korean pronunciation, the relation between the Korean and the Anglo-Saxon vernacular language is virtually non-existent until recent history. To this end, Koreans who wish to communicate effectively with English-speaking people should make an arduous and tireless effort to master the English language.

Caring for Autistic Child

by Dorothy Hong
Edited Article First Published in Spirit of y-Kan
Volume 8 Number 8, March 1998 Issue

Excerpts from Asbury Korean Methodist Bible Study Group fellowship time

I would like to share my volunteer experience with the Asbury Korean Group. I have done volunteer work ever since I was a teenager in high school. More recently, I do volunteer work through the Junior League of Bronxville. The Junior League of Bronxville is a woman's organization whose volunteer work in the local community is manifested in church, school, park and other community affairs.

I volunteer as a music therapist assistant for disabled children in a music therapy program every other Saturday. I was assigned to a girl who was diagnosed as having autism. Every Saturday morning I look after her helping her get through each session, by helping her play instruments and engage in group activities. I made observations about her in a note after each session. By the end of the semester I saw a noticeable improvement in her behavior though she was not completely cured. Witnessing progress and improvement has made all the difference in my life. I was glad that I was part of that progress in the child.

I learned yet another facet of Christian love as I poured my energy and care for that child. I found that a great thing about love is not necessarily feeling loved by someone nor someone's reciprocating your kind deeds, but rather in the very act of giving care and love to another. Loving that child gave me a feeling of joy and confidence. Such a good feeling has improved the quality of my life.

A Book Review of Don Oberdorfer's The Two Koreas

by Dorothy Hong
Edited Article First Published in Spirit of y-Kan
Volume 9 Number 9, May 1999 Issue

Don Oberdorfer writes about a contemporary history of North and South Korea in his book The Two Koreas. He writes "whatever the future holds, [for Koreas], it is likely to develop with high drama, intense emotion, and powerful impact." Mr. Oberdorfor brings his military and journalist experiences in his account of the most notable recent series of events on the Korean peninsula. His stories are filled with rich imageries, unforgettable quotes and easy to understand analyses.

A few things I know about Korea, he is accurate and many other historical events which I am not entirely clear about he conveys clear understanding to the readers and gives meanings to the sequence of events as they relate to the American foreign policy.

Each Korea with its own distinct "Ism" believes that it is the correct way to preserve Korea's prosperity and longevity. So far, South Korea has outpaced North Korea, most remarkably in the economic arena since the Korean War.

Russia, Japan, China and the United States had been major players in shaping the course of actions of Koreas. While Russia's influence has dwindled, Mainland China's influence will surely be felt both in North and South Koreas as Mainland China has already become an integral trading partner of South Korea. Japan continues to remain an intimate economic ally to South Korea. Since the division into North and South, South Korea believes that the foreign policy of each President elect of the United States of America determines the relative stability there.

The ninety's brought troubling news to America. These news seems particularly unsettling from a distance. In the mid 1990's North Korea was beset by natural calamities as they confronted flood of a "biblical proportion," famine and untimely death of Kim IL Sung, its demigod leader. At the same time, South Korea's front page news was saturated with bribery scandals and corruptions at the highest level of public offices.

South Korea is a reminder of the stature of America on the surface of the globe and for this reason it has been a keen interest to Americans notwithstanding the traditional geo-politics of Korea with its ancient natural neighbors who share land/sea boundaries, common culture and same skin color.

No Place Like ELM

by Dorothy Hong
Edited Article First Published in CrossRoads
Volume 14 Number 1, March 1999 Issue

For over twenty years the Korean Methodist Church & Institute has been the focus of my commitment to Christianity and the Korean American community. Over the years with the Church, I attended Sunday School, participated in the youth group, joined the young adult group of the main congregation, and more recently, attended the English Language Ministry ("ELM"). So for me, this church has been the center of my spiritual and social community.

Our church also was the base from which I expanded outward into the larger community. For instance, I worked with the local Korean community as a volunteer in various non-profit organizations. I participated in the youth ministry with Chinese and Japanese Americans in New York City. I used to go to Chinatown on Saturday mornings to attend Bible study class with fellow Asian high school students. After the class we used to go to a local Chinese restaurant and have noodle soup for lunch.

Looking back, the years in which I was part of the youth group were some of the most hectic and, at the same time, some of the most fulfilling. I remember the frantic phone calls with other members of our youth group throughout the year, planning our Sunday School agenda. We held bake sales and dance parties to raise funds for the church building. We had parties at each others' homes and saw Broadway shows. We made over five hundred decorative paper carnation pins for Mother's Day. Occasionally, we played volleyball and basketball with other Korean church youth groups in New Jersey. While I was the youth group president, we put on a musical theater production entitled <u>What If Jesus Christ Came to the World Today</u> featuring many of our group's talents. At one Christmas party, after singing together for hours, we felt so exhilarated and inspired that we went out into the snow-filled streets, knocked on neighbors' doors, and sang for them.

What was remarkable about my youth group days, as I reflect back on them, was that, despite the wonderful togetherness of our community of Korean Americans, the members did not expect to return to this Korean church or attend any other Korean church after we entered adulthood. We expected that we would be well integrated into American society, thinking that we would not have to deal with the language and cultural barriers that our parents had confronted; it did not occur to us that we would need or want a separate place of worship.

After I finished my studies and entered the job market, however, I began to think differently. The feeling of isolation became so pervasive, even though it was, admittedly, self-imposed, that I was thrilled to see ELM come into being. Although I made an effort to attend a non-ethnic church to take full advantage of American pluralism, I keep finding myself wanting to come back to ELM. Now that I have outgrown my naïve belief in a completely integrated America, I am so glad that there is a place like ELM.

Cheju Island

by Dorothy Hong
Edited Article First Published in Spirit of y-Kan
Volume 9 Number 11, July 1999 Issue

Cheju Island is situated in the southern most tip outside of the Korean peninsula. It is a place famous for its citrus farms because of the warm climate. It has been the primary choice for vacation, and, in particular, a popular destination for honeymooners in South Korea.

Visitors will immediately notice statutes of varying sizes of "Harubum" everywhere in the island. Its local folklore has it that this grandfatherly figure with big bulging eyes has served as a fertility sign for centuries. Of an equal importance is the legend of Sobul. The legend has it that Sobul was commissioned by Emperor of China who after unifying the entire China wanted a special herb to empower him with an eternal life. Sobul and his boys voyaged in a large vessel built from thousand year old trees in China and the first land of their refuge was Cheju Island. There, Sobul found the herb of eternal life, but went on to settle in Japan. His three other pious boys who journeyed with Sobul stayed in Cheju Island and married three virgin girls later sent by Sobul. The legend has it that the boys were known as the demigod leaders and their girls princesses.

The best way to tour the main island is to have a private car service for a day or two. The driver will direct you to each scenic spot and you can stay at each tourist attraction as long as you like, then go to a next place of interest with the same driver. Some of the places not to be missed are magnificent falls, caves with spectacular views of grotto and rock formations, coastal areas with natural rocks shaped like legendary animals from the bygone eras, and ranches with horses bred in Mongolian Warrior style.

Stores are open until late; you will find many patrons in book stores and restaurants until late into evenings. Local restaurants offer a wide range of cuisines, both Western and Korean. And the marinated barbecued port spare ribs are a must for lunch in this region.

The island on the whole looks like quintessential Korean villages and farms, but some parts of town are reminiscent of California shores and northern European villages, stemming from an influence from the sojourners from those parts of the world.

On Sexual Harassment

by Dorothy Hong

Edited Article First Published in Spirit of y-Kan
Volume 10 Number 1, October 1999 Issue

The phrase "sexual harassment" may conjure up a wide range of male-female mis-understandings in sexual nature and a varying degree of impermissible conducts. It can be as simple as an unwanted glance, leering, unwanted attention showered with words, touching, gesturing or gifts, or as pervasive as on-going every day routine conducts consisting of non-consensual sexual intercourse or sexual intercourse performed under duress.

Sexual harassment is not a romance, although there is an element of physical attraction involved. Sexual harassment is not a sabotage, although the victim may be able to prove decrease in productivity, feel malaise, or document other physical or emotional distress or ailments.

Sexual harassment may easily be condoned by the society because of the uncertainty and ambiguity of individual male-female psycho-dynamics. Women are taught to live with facts of life which include preparing their life with potentially confrontational meeting with "naughty" or "rough" boys. Women had traditionally been brought up with the belief that women may have brought on male responding to female in sexual nature, for instance, if she is scantily clad.

In reality, sexual harassment is a tort, a misconduct against women. It betrays male perpetrator's low image of women, a careless conduct, and an aggression or obsession with sexual conquests in inappropriate situations where, regardless of gender, individual is expected to master and practice a certain level of civility and tolerance in certain social situations.

As the case law evolves, court may look at the elements making up a sexual harassment charge. But, from the harassed prey's perspective if a woman feels harassed then she is harassed. Women may have a varying degree of tolerance.

Statistics show that women of color are more susceptible to harassment. Asian women, although assumed to be the most easily preyed upon, may be the least willing to file a sexual harassment incident. As much as they may agree that such conducts fall below the standard of conduct expected of a fellow citizen in those circumstances, they may easily confuse the incidents as overt acts of racism. As a result, Asian women do not give a sexual harassment claim a fair attention.

Korean Art at the MET

by Dorothy Hong
Edited Article First Published in Spirit of y-Kan
Volume 10 Number 2 November 1999 Issue

The Arts of Korea Gallery is the permanent site at the Asian arts section of the Metropolitan Museum of Art in New York City. It displays, on a rotating and thematic basis, the Metropolitan's collections as well as other Korean collections in the U.S., Korea and its neighboring countries. In the past, Korean arts had been held in high esteem in its immediate neighbors only. Recently, Korean arts have captured a wide appeal from the West as well.

The Korean arts illustrate the highest ideals of the Korean way of life, spanning from the worship of native gods and spirits, paganism, ancestor worship, and later Buddhism and Neo-Confucianism. Recurrent motifs and patterns on prints, furnitures, architectures and statutes show the Korean worship of various deities and practice of certain ethics. Widely seen animal prints such as deers, cranes and tigers are said to bring tranquility, power and good fortunes.

The Museum displays a small collection from Koryo dynasty's (918-1392) celebrated Celadons and Chosun dynasty's white porcelain and powder greenware. As a result of publication of artisan's techniques and continuous apprenticeship among those in the same trade, reproductions of most of ceramics of the bygone era are possible. However, there are a few types of ceramics which, aside from the actual ones preserved from the past, are irreplaceable because of the artisan's inability to disclose the techniques. Most of these ceramics displayed may be seen in Korean stores of varying range of prestige and price. In the amateur's eye, however, these ceramics may seem like those generally found in a Korean family's living room, except the ones in the Museum look a little worn out.

The earliest earthenware of the Neolithic on display followed by those during the Three Kingdom period (57B.C.E.-666 C.E.) originated from the Eurasian steppe, just as the people themselves had. Since then, Korean arts have developed into a distinctive tradition within the Oriental arts, belonging in the same categories as that of China and Japan, with a hint of difference in the focus and the size of grandeur. The classic Korean arts, which were influenced primarily by the Chinese courtly arts, were thereafter transplanted to Japan, who were able to continue the same tradition in its own unique brand in the Oriental arts.

Fiction section

✦

Three (3) Short Stories

Dead Person Does Not Speak

by Dorothy Hong

In a small college town surrounded by nowherevilles a curse has subdued the vitality of the community, making them meek. For their natural passions have led them astray, making them oblivious to sublimation, leaving their descendants painfully aware of their sins. Those soldiers who chose to deny their history, too, have come to feel guilt. Guilt as their sole guidance in their course of actions, they grudgingly learn to share the ghost story of a young Korean college student.

The legend of Nam, Haye Ryun, the ghost, has come to haunt the living, persistently reminding a few chosen living that they have the duty to vindicate the ghost by seeking the truth. Picking her medium with utmost care, Miss Nam has appeared unexpectedly to recount her blood-curdling story.

On one breezy spring night devoid of humidity, Miss Nam was burnt to death. The entire house in which she had resided was burnt to the ground. A marked man appeared out of nowhere unobtrusively dressed in skin tight black which blended with the color of the night, leaked and poured gasoline around the house, splashing them on the four sides of the house, and with a stroke of match caused a spark, a bright flame, soon swiftly covering the house in full blaze. Unfortunately, the dry climate was conducive to the quick spread of fire. The residents of the house were rudely awakened by the smell of the fire and black smoke quickly soaring from the house. All of the neighbors had managed to escape the fire somehow. Miss Nam tried to get out of her room, but the door was jammed. "Hurry up!" a neighbor shouted frantically.

The residents in their pajamas and bath robes quickly did a head count, and noticed that Miss Nam was the only missing person from the house now consumed by blazing fire.

A handful of passersby were drawn to the brilliant burst of fire. They, however, were transfixed there watching the fire and betrayed indifference muttering, "How dreadfully funny that such a special house should burn so brightly." One of them rushed down the hill to alert the townies. There was no fire department in this town. Rather, townies volunteered whenever they received notices of fire. It took almost two years to build this house, yet within an hour the house was barely recognizable, sides of the house completely covered in black soot and leaving only the framework intact.

Miss Nam was all alone in her room, feeling trapped. In this state of utter helplessness Miss Nam tried to maintain her calm, quietly preparing herself to the impending death. The spectators expected to hear screams of pain, but all they heard instead was the crackling sound of fire.

The next day, an accidental fire was reported. Everybody blamed the dry weather. No effort was made to investigate the possibility of arson. At the town meeting, the place where the house once stood was decided to become a private parking lot. A college official sent a letter to Miss Nam's parents in Korea regrettably informing them of their daughter's disappearance. The fire story was hushed for policy reasons. It turns out that not only was Miss Nam the only racial minority who had resided in the burnt house, but she had been the only Korean student in the entire student body on campus. Nam's parents were appalled. "She was so looking forward to studying with American children there," they lamented. They and a wave of other Koreans thereafter flew from Korea, determined to search Miss Nam's body that was discarded somewhere in this town.

Thinking that Miss Nam was forever put to silence, immediately after confirmation of her death, her neighbors began to talk about her without restraint and maliciously. "She was too pure, she did not fit in here," they would say. "She was really crazy," said another knowingly, "She was delusional; and she kept hearing the voice of dead Andrew whom she wanted to marry." They started to giggle uncontrollably. Andrew was a fellow Asian male student who was murdered the day after he had attended a co-ed party. Two witnesses at the party said Andrew was feeling his oat and began making a pass at a pudgy blonde co-ed student. Andrew denied this, indicating that he had a blurred vision there because he misplaced his eyeglasses earlier that day and came to the party without wearing one. The school official denied any connection between the party incident and

Andrew's murder, but did indicate that fellow students may have been jealous because Andrew was doing well in school and he was not on scholarship.

The legend has it that the spirit of Miss Nam has decided to stay in this town, instead of re-uniting in spirit with her loved one, Andrew, turning the place into a rainy town. It seems to rain endlessly during the spring time. "You can't live here without an umbrella, " an orientation counselor advised an incoming freshman. "Do you mean an umbrella, a devise for protection against rain or an organization encompassing diverse groups?" quipped the wide-eyed freshman. The orientation counselor was speechless.

As the freshman was walking by the gorge she felt a few drops of rain which tasted like Miss Nam's tear. The townies said each time a lie was uttered Miss Nam would begin to cry and her tears would fall down to the earth. "Unless the truth shall be told this town will continue to be rainy. Pass it on," said a townie.

A Less Formidable Foe

by Dorothy Hong

A young female lawyer comes home from a job interview and enters her apartment. "How was your interview at Foster & Palmer?" asked Arthur. Arthur's wife, Susan looked like she was going to cry as her lips trembled. "What happened, honey? You look terribly upset," inquired Arthur gently rubbing Susan's back in an effort to soothe her. "A Spick looked at me," said Susan. "How did he look at you?" asked Arthur. "He was giving me signals. I felt dirty. I still feel dirty. Not even a million showers would take away the dirt I feel inside me." Said Susan. Arthur tried to remain nonchalant, but inquired," What is his name?" Susan responded curtly," George Gomez," said Susan. "I'm going to have him taken to dry cleaners and killed!" shouted Arthur. "How? You can go to jail for that," pleaded Susan.

"I have friends. We are close…very close. They owe me some favors. I'll take care of this once and for all," said Arthur adamantly. "I can't believe some fresh off the boat Spick had all these nasty designs on you. They are disturbing the status quo. They are nothing but trouble, I tell you," Arthur was emphatic.

Susan finished her diet Coke and looked straight in the eye of Arthur and said, "Look, let's forget that. I'm not even sure that I got the job. I want the job but I'll bet that those Gooks have better chance of landing on those spots than I do. They are all menace to the society. They are rude; they don't wait their turn. Before you know I'll be out on the street, eating off of scraped chewing gum those Niggers spat on to the ground." Arthur gestured as if he were a Prosecutor during his summation and said, "That is not the point. He's got some nerve leering at you. Next thing you know, he'll not only step all over you, but he will be pouncing all over you. Just the thought of it is disgusting. I'm not going to let it slide this time. I've had it enough. Enough is enough." "I'm going to bed. I'm tired." Susan yawned and headed toward bathroom to brush her teeth.

Five days later Susan got a call from the hiring partner of Foster & Palmer indicating that Susan will be able to join the firm as a second year associate. She was able to join the rank of second year because in the previous year she had served as a clerk to a judge in California. After she heard the news she felt compelled to drive out to the Bronx to go shopping at Loehmann's. There she purchased fifteen suits, five dresses, four pair of stockings and a couple of blouses. She may have overdone it, but she felt better about herself afterwards. She then drove back to the City, had a California roll and miso soup at a Japanese bistro for lunch and went to a beauty parlor to get her hair cut. Her new haircut unabashedly revealed her ears and neck. This was the new "corporate" look she decided. Her top layer of hair swung in the air like Dorothy Hamill in the "Short & Sassy" shampoo commercial. She ran her fingers through her hair to feel the freshly cut hair, feeling in her fingers the soft edge of bristled hair. She felt boyish. She imagined herself in her first day of work. She was stirred during the interview. She still feels stirred. But she did not like him, she decided. He was gross. He was Latino. He was a boy-man of color. So, he was from a different planet, habitually orbiting around a different set of women, Hispanic women. Then Susan thought of her husband, Arthur. Her husband's response was not unexpected. She then pondered how many Hispanic girls had been taken advantage by white men, judging from her husband's almost Pavlovian response.

Susan entered the reception area of the law firm of Foster & Palmer the following week. Susan was greeted by George Gomez and she followed him to his cramped and cluttered office. "How are you, sir?" asked Susan. "Tired. But, I have a bit of a news. Starting today…" George's sentence was interrupted by a telephone ring. "George Gomez speaking." Pause. "Hello, Hello" George then hung up. "I'm glad you came into my office. There had been some changes around here. You will be reporting to…" A telephone rang again. "George Gomez speaking, hello." George then sighed and hung up. "Please speak with Mr. Sohn, down the corridor. He'll be your supervisor instead." Susan smiled involuntarily as she was dumbfounded. "I see," said Susan pensively. "Welcome aboard, Mrs. Buckingham," said George Gomez forcing a smile on his face.

Susan then walked into Mr. Sohn's office. Mr. Sohn's office was filled with diplomas and certificates. He had gone to Seoul National University Law School, but received his LLM degree from Harvard Law School. He is a member of Bar of South Korea, New York, New Jersey and California. It looked a bit ridiculous to line up his degrees in the most conspicuous area in his office space, but for some reason Susan nevertheless had difficulty trying to convince herself that he was a competent lawyer. Mr. Sohn had to repeat a few times a number of items because Susan had failed to understand the assignment. Susan could not understand his accent. Susan could immediately detect the nasal intonation so typical of Oriental people. Furthermore, his deflections and pronunciation of certain words sounded like his tongue had been paralyzed by anesthesia. His rapid speed of speech and his brisk mannerism seemed incongruous with his enunciation patterns. He comes from a different culture, Susan decided. She quickly dismissed her distracting image of Mr. Sohn being crucified with his tongue completely pulled out from his gut in front of his native aristocrat's court.

Susan then looked at Mr. Sohn's neck. There was something soft and silky about his white shirt. His white shirt did not seem that white, maybe because, Susan thought, he is not white. Certainly, it was not the kind of crisp and starchy white shirt that Susan had been seeing in the hallways and corridors all morning in the office. It was not just his white shirt that seemed little out of place. Mr. Sohn's long torso and short legs seemed comical as if a disabled person escaped out of asylum and was made socially useful in a circus. He must spend a fortune in the tailor's shop for alterations, Susan mused. There was something odd and somber about the way his coarse and straight black hair blended with his dark suit. Feeling was decidedly different from the ashen and powdery blonde look of other uniformly tall leggy white attorneys in the law firm.

Susan deliberately thought of other differences which set Mr. Sohn apart and isolated him from the social fabric of the law firm. Basically, Susan felt left out working with a Korean partner working on Asian matters. She wanted to be part of the mainstream, if not the core of the law firm culture.

Mr. Sohn's wear and tear about him lent her a feeling of familiarity and superiority. Yet her feeling of euphoria dissipated abruptly because of Mr. Sohn's icy piercing sloe-eyed glance. It had just occurred to Susan that not once had Mr. Sohn looked at her in the face. Each time Susan tried to make an eye contact, Mr. Sohn looked away. And then he casted his gaze downward. Susan felt self-conscious after a few attempts. Susan instinctively wanted to feel confident about her sexuality, but her efforts were futile when confronted one to one with an Asian man. Susan felt agitated and was silently trembling.

After an initial meeting with Mr. Sohn, Susan felt so humiliated that she rushed to the Personnel office. There she poured her heart out to her equal, a white personnel. "I'm getting too close to Mr. Sohn, if you know what I mean. I can't control him. He touched my hand and I...I can't go into it. Let me recount. The first encounter was a dangerous one, which I'm not going to get too graphic with anyone, not even to my husband." Susan confided and began to cry. Susan then went back to her office, feeling refreshed and confident.

At home that evening Arthur asked, "How was your first day at the office?" Susan longing for her man's hug whispered, "I was assigned to a real Chauvinist pig Oriental man. He does not belong in the 21st century. Not only that he has a series language and cultural problems. That Kori should not even be in the office. He is a real Gook. He completely dehumanized me," Susan spoke in slow and soft tone. "You should talk to the hiring partner. Let us not forget to nip in the bud. Don't let a Vietcong step all over you. They are Yellow Peril. They should go back to where they come from! Or else they'll end up being a chopped up meat and their bones, old English china platters." Arthur felt clever and for the first time in years he felt like a real WASP.

Next day Susan went to see the hiring partner, Mr. R. Everybody in the firm calls him Mr. R. because his last name is too long and difficult to pronounce. Susan's first impression of Mr. R. was that he looked like he had been a basketball player in his youthful days. He still looks as though he works out at health clubs regularly. "Uh hum," Susan cleared her throat. "I would like to file a complaint." She continued holding her breath. "Mr. Sohn has a serious cultural adjustment problems. I cannot work with him. He does not even look at a person he is speaking with. But, when I looked at him straight in the eye to make a point, he was turning red, feverish, burning with desire. He cannot control himself. I'm afraid of my own safety. You know, as an expecting WASP woman...we should look after our own interest for change." Mr. R. wiped his glasses as to rid smudges and then looked at her signaling to continue in the same vain as if he is in a pep rally. "Mr. Sohn makes absolutely no eye contact. Is he shy? I think he is shy. I'm afraid he is hopelessly in love with me. How can I break his heart and tell him that I'm happily married. This should be a firm—on going concern. I shall keep abreast of each development." Susan gestured in the Boy Scout fashion. "Thank you, Mrs. Buckingham. You know my door is always open for you," said Mr. R.

Two weeks later Arthur came home looking distressed. "How was your day, Art?" asked Susan. "I'm running into some problems with my arrangement." Arthur sighed. "What arrangement? What are you talking about?" asked Susan. Arthur started to feel betrayed and was livid. "I gave those Niggers everything they have. What more can they ask for?" Susan was still thinking about Mr. Sohn, while her husband was making a reference to the Latino attorney. Susan then burst out after realizing that the Korean attorney may be suspecting something, "What is it? Is it those uppity yellow lesbians? I'll have them raped and murdered if they don't submit themselves to you!" stammered Susan. "Calm down, Susan. Those Niggers are not listening to me. Not only that, they want to get paid for taking care of our Latino problem," lamented Arthur. Susan involuntarily doing a pelvic twist felt confused and then murmured, "I want her raped and murdered, I'm sexy, I'm white."

Susan then took off her sweater and wiggled her behind and started to strip tease in front of her husband, "I'm ready!" Susan looked at Arthur tearfully. "I'm not in the mood, Put your clothes back on. What happened to your pubic hairs? You seem to have lost some." Susan was indignant that nothing was going right and she couldn't make anyone do anything the way she wanted. Noticing the hostile glare from his wife Arthur pushed her away in an effort to subdue her. Susan shouted, "I'm not taking 'No' from you. I'm not taking 'No.' I'm not taking no from you tonight!" Susan was emphatic. Arthur then slapped her. Susan was fuming. She dashed into the kitchen, grabbed a kitchen knife and stormed out of there to the bedroom and came near her husband to profoundly illustrate her point and to retaliate against battery. She stood there for a brief period, panting, with a knife hungry for his affection and longing for his acquiescence. Arthur tried to her grab her arms. "Who is the bastard who did this to you! Talk to me. I'm not your enemy. Who made you this way!" pleaded Arthur. Susan successfully resisted and tried to free herself. After gulping down a whiff of air into her lungs, she plunged the knife into his heart. Arthur died. Susan was down on the floor in a pool of blood beside her dead husband weeping.

Meeting at the Clinic

by Dorothy Hong

"I think that guy likes you. He keeps coming back to see you," nudged Nancy Lange, a fellow sandwich maker at Burke & Burke. "Thank you, but I think it's because the food is good here," said Bella Russko as she watched a tall Asian man walk out of the store. Nancy didn't know that Bella had been dating this man for two months. "Is he Eurasian? A mixed breed?" asked Nancy. "No, actually, he's Korean, " responded Bella. "I think he is mixed. I have my sources," said Nancy knowingly. Nancy then added, "I am having a little get together at my place on Friday, why don't you come. Bring something to drink," said Nancy cordially.

That Friday evening Bella showed up at Nancy's crammed apartment with a bottle of red wine. There was a loud music and a throng looking somewhat drunk, talking freely with drinks and cigarettes in their hands. Nancy introduced Bella to a burly Slavic man. The Slavic man who introduced himself as Mick was practically spending the whole evening with Bella, cornering her with his arms and hands. Mick was mesmerized by Bella's blonde hair and green eyed face and petite figure with large bosoms. Bella was beginning to feel uncomfortable as Mick was touching various parts of Bella's body both intentionally and inadvertently as he engaged in a lively conversation with Bella and another woman.

Mick volunteered to drive Bella home. Inside his car as he exited from the highway and parked his car in an abandoned dead end street Mick proceeded to rape Bella. After the rape is complete, as Mick was slowly coming out of the state of rapture, he realized that Bella had not consented to the sexual intercourse. When he tried to talk to Bella, she pushed him aside instead and with anew found strength she had not yet realized, managed to run out of the car and away from the dark alley and headed toward a well lit main street.

Three months have elapsed since the party. Bella continued to work at the upscale Deli shop. And she was still dating the same Korean man. Bella's Korean boyfriend, John Rhee, was beginning to get worried over Bella's taciturn. He tried to engage her in a frank exchange but Bella seemed resolute in keeping the affair to herself. One evening Bella asked "Why would you date me instead of another Korean girl with nice smooth skin like the outer whites of poached egg?" "Is anything or anyone bothering you," asked John. At this point John realized that Bella was in a serious trouble. He was so consumed with anxiety that when Bella put her hand on her stomach, he wanted to eat her. Bella was alarmed and declared, "I never want to see you again." She left him.

Thereafter Bella realized that she was pregnant. She knew that the sire was Mick's since her relationship with John had been a platonic one. Since Bella and John drifted apart and she had not seen John for a while Bella quickly made an appointment with the Planned Parenthood to get an abortion. Because Bella detested Mick, she did not contact him about her decision. Nor did she let John know about this. He does not need to know this kind of shame and violence, Bella decided.

As Bella was quietly sitting in the waiting room of the Planned Parenthood clinic she noticed an Asian woman sitting there reading the New York Post. Bella decided to sit next to the Asian woman because she felt that what she was going through was not unique, but there were others who were similarly situated. Bella asked the Asian woman what kind of examination she is here for. The Asian woman responded, "Abortion, although I'm five months pregnant. After this I can get a permanent job," the Asian woman said as a matter of fact, "Who wants to pay attention to damaged good in work place!" She then crossed her legs. "Why do you say that?" asked Bella. "Who wants a damaged good," murmured the Asian girl with abundant and strikingly jet black hair covering her shoulders. For no reason Bella felt remorseful as she heard these words. Bella wanted to cry but she did not have any tear left. All of sudden, she felt exhausted.

"How did you get pregnant?" asked Bella desperately seeking a common bond between them. The Asian woman responded, "I have a very nice personality, at least that is what people tell me. I live with my parents and my father lost his job recently, and we had trouble making ends meet. It was for an efficiency reason that he was let go. So I guess I was an easy target." "What does that have to do with your being here?" asked Bella. "Maybe an act of retaliation. My white girl-friend was going around showing photo of her black and blue bruises and the next minute, you know, like a wild forest fire, rumor gets around that my father had raped her. My mother says that must have been a miraculous act because he can't do it even with Viagra. So you see this is my punishment." Bella instinctively knew that the Asian girl had experienced orgasm and judging from her bony body it was quite possible that she was suffering from amenorhea. The Asian girl then summed up, "I have a bit of advise for you. You should use a false name for this kind of operation. For privacy reasons. Nobody needs to know this kind of thing," she looked searchingly at Bella. "Whose name did you use?" inquired Bella. At that point the Asian woman's boyfriend appeared. He had a lanky figure and looked like a Southeast Asian man judging from his slightly sunken eyes.

"You friend, Alice?" asked the boyfriend. The Asian woman didn't say anything. Bella then asked, "She told me. Does the Police know about this?" asked Bella. The Asian man then sat down and drew a long breath. Bella then detected a fire in the young man's eyes and fury in his voice, "No. It's my fault. Normally I wear eyeglasses, but starting about a couple of months ago I started wearing contact lens. But one morning I was too lazy to put on contact lens to work because I had overslept, so I went back to my eyeglasses that day. At work I briefly took off my glasses to wipe off dust and as I was doing so I must have been looking at a female co-worker. She told her apartment mate that I was giving her signals and next minute her temperamental Greek Jewish boyfriend sodomized me and raped my girlfriend." Bella's jaw dropped upon hearing this. "I'm very sorry to hear that," Bella said solemnly. Then Bella suddenly got up and left the Clinic.

After making proper arrangements Bella purchased an air plane ticket to Poland and made plans to stay there until the arrival of baby at which point she would put up for an adoption there. She packed her stuff, and wrote a note to Nancy, the sandwich maker at Burke and Burke. Bella thanked Nancy profusely for inviting her to the party, but because of variety of reasons for which Nancy is not at fault, she is going to Austria to commit suicide because she had been in unrequited love with Mick, a man she had loved for the first time in her life. She thanked again for all the hospitality in America. She dropped the mail in her neighborhood mailbox and then took a cab to the JFK Airport.

Upon arrival at the departure gate at the JFK Airport, John, the Korean guy, came out of nowhere and grabbed Bella in the arm, "Don't leave me. I heard everything. We can raise the child together. I understand." Bella responded, "Leave me alone," and speedily headed toward the plane.

0-595-28390-X